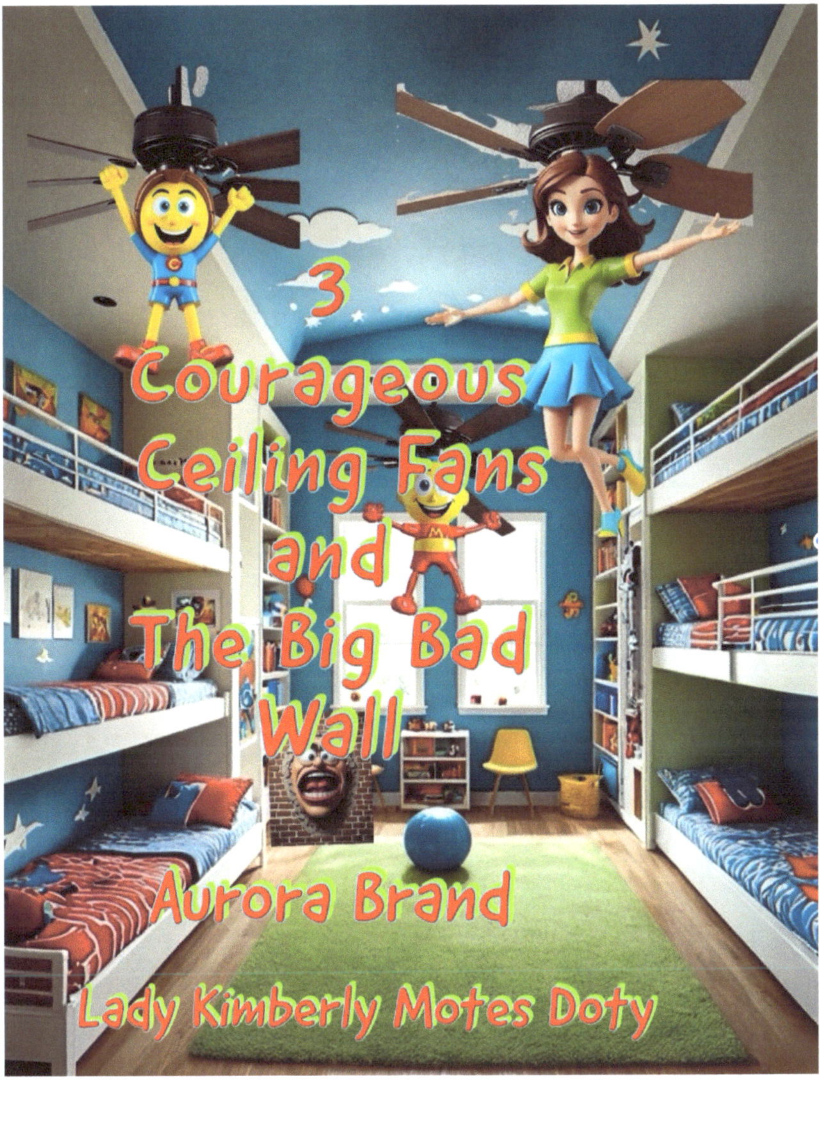

3 Courageous Ceiling Fans and The Big Bad Wall

Aurora Brand

Lady Kimberly Motes Doty

3 Courageous Ceiling Fans and the Big Bad Wall

Aurora Brand
Lady Kimberly Motes Doty

ISBN   979-8-3302-0847-0 (paperback book) Ingram

ISBN   979-8-3302-0848-7 (digital ebook) Ingram

ISBN   979-8-3341-7453-5 (paperback book) Amazon

ASIN   B0D8Z35TMJ   (digital ebook) Amazon

ISBN   (audio book)

ISBN   (hardcover book)

Lady Kimberly Industries LLC

15019 Madeira Way, #86174

Madeira Beach, Florida 33708-9998

www.LadyKimberlyIndustries.com

https://mybook.to/LadyKimberlyBooks

3 Courageous Ceiling Fans and the Big Bad Wall

By:

Aurora Brand
Lady Kimberly Motes Doty

Once upon a time, in a world full of emotions, there lived three courageous ceiling fans named

Max,

Bella,

&

Charlie.

C
M

They were not your ordinary ceiling fans -

they could think,

they could feel,

and they could dream.

I have always wanted my house ...
My house will have ...
When I have my own house ...

Inspired by their favorite storybook, they decided to build their own houses.

I love soft pillows & blankets!

Max,
the adventurous fan,
wanted his house to be cozy
and unique.

"I love soft pillows and
blankets" he told his ceiling
fan friends.

He gathered colorful blankets and soft pillows to create a warm and inviting space.

I like to recycle!

Bella,

with her practical nature, decided to build her house with a sturdy roof made of recycled materials, ensuring durability and protection.

Bella told her ceiling fan friends, "I like to recycle so my house will be made of recycled materials."

She gathered sturdy recycled materials to ensure her home was durable and provided good protection too.

My house
will be
safe &
secure!

Charlie,
the wise fan,
wanted his house to be safe
and secure.

"My house will be safe and
secure" Charlie told his ceiling
fan friends.

He chose to build his house with solid bricks and installed a state-of-the-art security system to keep any intruders at bay.

Little did they know, lurking nearby was the big bad wall.

The big bad wall was known for its destructive ways.

The big bad wall also had a reputation for tearing down houses ...

and causing chaos wherever it went.

One fateful day, the big bad wall spotted the three little ceiling fan houses and approached them with a wicked grin.

"Ceiling fan, Ceiling fan, Let me in or I'll whack your houses down!" it bellowed, thinking it would be an easy task.

We're not
giving
up our
homes!

But the three little ceiling fans were not about to give up their homes without a fight.

"We're not giving up our homes" they told the big bad ceiling fan.

Not by
the power
of my
spinning
blades!
M

Max, the first to face the big bad wall, stood his ground.

"Not by the power of my spinning blades!" he declared defiantly.

However, his cozy house made of blankets was no match for the wall's strength, and it crumbled to the ground.

Not by
the force
of the
wind!

Next, it was Bella's turn to confront the big bad wall.

She bravely stood in front of her house with the sturdy roof and declared, "Not by the force of the wind!"

But alas, the wall's power was too great, and Bella's house was demolished.

Finally, it was Charlie's turn. He stood proudly in front of his secure brick house, ready to defend it.

ACCESS DENIED

As the big bad wall approached, Charlie's security system sprang into action.

Alarms blared, lights flashed, and a powerful gust of wind was unleashed, pushing the wall back.

ACCESS DENIED

The wall tried relentlessly to break through, but Charlie's house stood strong.

With a final mighty gust, the big bad wall was flung far away, all the way to North Carolina by way of the South Pole!

The Big Bad Wall would never bother the little fans again.

Yippee!
The Big
Bad Wall
is gone
forever!

Max, Bella, and Charlie celebrated their victory, knowing they had outsmarted the big bad wall.

Max & Bella rebuilt their homes.

M

From that day on, Max, Bella, and Charlie lived happily ever after in their resilient and secure houses.

The 3 Courageous Ceiling fans continued to circulate the air, bringing comfort to all who encountered them.

My house
will have
When
I have
my own
house

Their tale became a legend, reminding everyone that with determination and the right defenses, even the strongest challenges can be overcome.

And so, the story of the three little ceiling fans and the big bad wall spread far and wide, inspiring others to build their own houses with strength, security, and a touch of creativity.

The End.

About the Author
Aurora Brand

   Meet Aurora Brand, a spirited and visionary 9-year-old girl whose exceptional creativity sets her apart. Her boundless imagination captivates not only her adoring younger brother Cade, but also her loving Mommy Tamara, her wise Papaw John, and her cherished Mamaw Lady Kimberly. Nestled in the vibrant landscapes of southern Florida, Aurora hones her artistic talents by delighting her family with her unique creations.

Aurora's artistic prowess knows no bounds, as she effortlessly navigates between the realms of imaginative artistry and captivating storytelling. With a pen in one hand and a paintbrush in the other, she is destined to become one of the rising stars in the realm of young writers. The world eagerly awaits as she blossoms and flourishes in the years to come.

In the exciting debut of her first book in her new children's series, "The Whimsical World of the Little - 125+ Silly Variations That Will Make You Squeal with Laughter"," Aurora unveils a groundbreaking approach to teaching children invaluable life lessons. Aurora ingeniously weaves non-traditional elements such as ceiling fans and walls into her narrative. This extraordinary collection brings together over 125 whimsical and hilarious variations of the classic story, guaranteed to tickle your funny bone and ignite your imagination.

In this imaginative world, the "littles" take on new adventures, encounter peculiar characters, and face unexpected challenges in the most playful and entertaining ways. From pirates sailing the bacon seas to astronauts exploring the hamisphere, each story will transport you to a world filled with laughter, surprises, and endless joy. Join the mischievous trio as they build their houses with unconventional materials like marshmallows, bubblegum, and even cotton candy. Encounter wacky versions of the big bad wolf, who might just turn out to be a big bad wall, a goofball or a big bad hipster with a penchant for organic kale. These imaginative twists and turns will keep you giggling and guessing until the very end.Through these unconventional characters, she imparts essential values such as strength, security, and creativity.

Aurora's stories are a breath of fresh air, infusing traditional tales with her own unique perspective. Her ingenious storytelling not only entertains but also ignites the spark of curiosity and imagination within young minds. As her stories reach the hands of eager readers, they will embark on a transformative journey, discovering the power of unconventional wisdom and the limitless possibilities that lie within their own imaginations.

In Aurora Brand, we find an extraordinary young talent whose radiant spirit and innovative approach will undoubtedly leave an indelible mark on the literary world. Let us celebrate her remarkable achievements and eagerly anticipate the wonders she will create in the years ahead.

Lady Kimberly Motes Doty

Get ready to be inspired and motivated by the incredible works of Lady Kimberly Motes Doty. With a passion for helping others and a wealth of knowledge in various fields, Lady Kimberly's books are a treasure trove of wisdom and guidance.

In her role as a minister, Lady Kimberly assists individuals in finding their spiritual path, offering solace and support along the way. As a life coach, she empowers others to live their best lives and unlock their true potential. Her expertise as a natural health specialist ensures that readers gain valuable insights into taking care of their bodies and maintaining optimal well-being.

Lady Kimberly's love for writing shines through in every page of her books. Through her words, she shares her profound wisdom and uplifting messages with readers, inspiring them to embrace positive change and discover their own inner strength.

When she's not immersed in her various roles, Lady Kimberly cherishes spending quality time with her family, finding joy and inspiration in their presence.

From "A Children's Guide to a Godly Way of Life" to "Treasure Hunters, A Beachcombing Adventure," Lady Kimberly's books cover a wide range of topics that cater to readers of all ages and interests. Whether you're seeking spiritual guidance, organizational tools, or thought-provoking insights, her books have something special to offer.

With each turn of the page, you'll be captivated by Lady Kimberly's unique writing style and her ability to connect with readers on a deep and personal level. Her books are not just words on a page; they are transformative experiences that will leave you feeling inspired, motivated, and ready to embark on your own journey of self-discovery.

Don't miss out on the opportunity to enrich your life with the wisdom and inspiration found within Lady Kimberly Motes Doty's books. Get your hands on these remarkable works today and unlock the potential within you to live a fulfilling and empowered life.

https://ladykimberlyindustries.com

https://mybook.to/LadyKimberlyBooks

More Lady Kimberly Children's Books

"If The Alphabet Grew Out of The Sea v2" - Almost 600 pages of mazes, word searches and fun facts about sea animals on an exciting Sea Adventure!

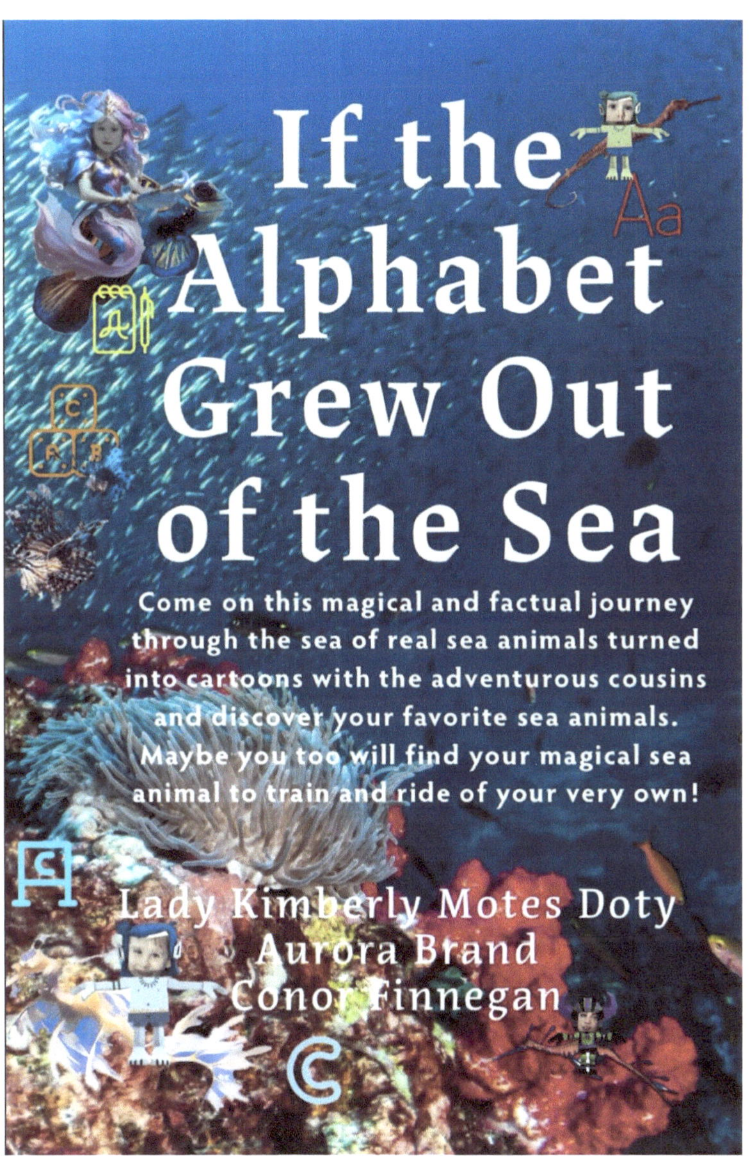

"If the Alphabet Grew Out of The Sea" V1 - in English, French & Spanish

Conor's
Magical
Treasure
Hunt
Get ready for an enchanting adventure
with Conor and his wise grandmother,
Mimi, in this inspiring tale of love,
discovery, and the magic of the sea.
Join them as they set off on a treasure
hunt to find the perfect Conch shell,
rumored to possess a magical sound.
Lady Kimberly Motes Doty

Treasure Hunters
A Beachcombing Adventure
Lady Kimberly Motes Doty

Enchanted
Seashell
A Magical Beach Adventure
Lady Kimberly Motes Doty

A children's book series written by children for children!

"The Whimsical World of the Littles: 125+ Silly Variations That Will Make You Squeal with Laughter"

Welcome to "The Whimsical World of the Littles, a 125+ Silly Variations That Will Make You Squeal with Laughter"! Get ready to embark on a delightful journey through the enchanting tales like you've never experienced before. This extraordinary collection brings together over 125 whimsical and hilarious variations of the classic story, guaranteed to tickle your funny bone and ignite your imagination.

In this imaginative world, the littles take on new adventures, encounter peculiar characters, and face unexpected challenges in the most playful and entertaining ways. From pirates sailing the bacon seas to astronauts exploring the hamisphere, each story will transport you to a world filled with laughter, surprises, and endless joy.

Join the mischievous trio as they build their houses with unconventional materials like pillows, marshmallows, bubblegum, and even cotton candy. Encounter wacky versions of the big bad wolf, who might just turn out to be a big bad wall, a goofball or a big bad hipster with a penchant for organic kale. These imaginative twists and turns will keep you giggling and guessing until the very end.

3
Courageous
Ceiling Fans
and
The Big Bad
Wall

Aurora Brand

Lady Kimberly Motes Doty

Candlestorm
Chronicles
Cade Brand
Lady Kimberly Motes Doty

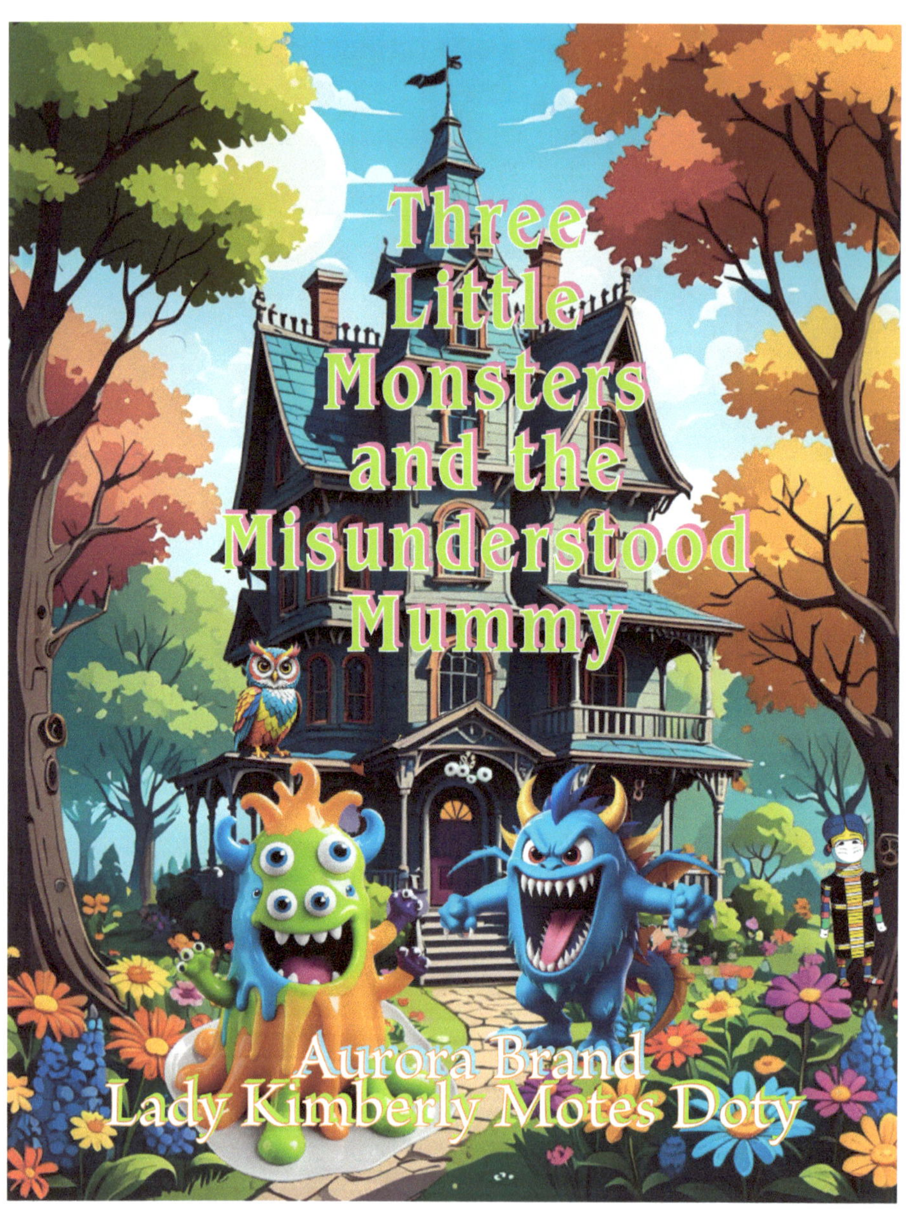
Three
Little
Monsters
and the
Misunderstood
Mummy

Aurora Brand
Lady Kimberly Motes Doty

Good-Bye! Come back and read with us again!

Toodles!

I can't wait to see you again!

See ya!
We'll really miss you! Come back soon!

Aurora Brand & Lady Kimberly Motes Doty

www.ingramcontent.com/pod-product-compliance
Lightning Source LLC
Chambersburg PA
CBHW040922110726
48006CB00001B/34